Vocabulary chart

Title	Vocabulary	Sounds	Bookband Level
Making a Space Shuttle	make, off, take, back, more, when, them, again, from, now, what	'oo' (pull, look) 'oo' (moon, booster) 'or' (orbit, orbiter)	8 purple
Things that Sting	what, off, your, some, may, their, very, more, down, one, another, out, make, little, time, surviving, dangerous	'air' (their) 'or' (warm, your, claws) 'er' (curtain)	9 gold
Sport Then and Now	new, now, old, ran, some, been, have, people, these, more, made, first, very, white, over, were	'or' (sport, worn) 'er' (skirt, player)	10 white
Fire	put, out, when, not, were, people, these, many, down, water, half	'er' (worst) 'i' (fire, lightning)	9 gold
Glorious Mud	mud, with, make, made, water, out, about, love, some, white, one, have, new, from, what	'oo' (could) 'er' (water, layer, bird) 'or' (record) 'oo' (cool, classroom)	9 gold
What Do You Want To Be?	who, want, some, people, these, more, about, make move, there, would, new, many, help, take, after	'oo' (would, could, look) 'er' (work, teacher, person) 'oo' (tools, boots)	8 purple

Teaching objectives

	Teacher's Notes			Guided Reading Cards
	Speaking and listening	Reading	Writing	Reading
Making a Space Shuttle				
Scotland	Listening/Talking Level A/B	Level A/B	Level A/B	Level A/B
N. Ireland	Activities a, f, g Outcomes a, b, e, g, h	Activities a, b Outcomes b, c, d, e, f, h	Opportunities a Outcomes b	Activities a, b Outcomes f, h
Wales	Oracy Range 1, 3 Skills 1, 2, 5	Range 1, 2, 3 Skills 1, 2, 4	Range 1, 2, 4 Skills 1, 2, 5	Range 1, 2, 3 Skills 2, 4
NC/NLS Y2T2	2e	T18 T19 S3 S9 W5	T21	T20 S7 W5
Things that Sting				
Scotland	Listening/Talking Level A/B	Level A/B	Level A/B	Level A/B
N. Ireland	Activities a, f, g Outcomes a, b, e, g, h	Activities a, b Outcomes b, c, d, e, f, h	Opportunities a Outcomes a, b, c	Activities a, b Outcomes b, c, d, f
Wales	Oracy Range 1, 3 Skills 1, 2, 5	Range 1, 2 Skills 1, 2, 4	Range 1, 2, 4 Skills 1, 4, 7	Range 1, 2, 3 Skills 1, 2, 4
NC/NLS Y2T2	2e	T18 S4 W5	S2	S7 W2 W5
Sport Then and Now				
Scotland	Listening/Talking Level A/B	Level A/B	Level A/B	Level A/B
N. Ireland	Activities a, f, g Outcomes a, b, c, e, g, h	Activities a, b Outcomes b, c, d, e, f, h	Opportunities a Outcomes b, h, i	Activities a, b Outcomes b, c, d, f
Wales	Oracy Range 1, 3 Skills 1, 2, 5	Range 1, 2, 3, 4 Skills 1, 2, 4	Range 1, 2, 4 Skills 1, 3, 4, 8	Range 1, 2, 3 Skills 1, 2
NC/NLS Y2T2	2e	T7 T16 S2 S10	T2 T20	T2 S1 W10
Fire				
Scotland	Listening/Talking Level A	Level A/B	Level A/B	Level A/B
N. Ireland	Activities a, f, g, i Outcomes a, b, c, d, e, g, i	Activities a, b Outcomes b, c, d, e, f, h	Opportunities a Outcomes b	Activities a, b Outcomes b, c, f, h
Wales	Oracy Range 1, 2, 3 Skills 1, 2, 3, 4, 5, 6	Range 1, 2, 3 Skills 1, 2, 4	Range 1, 2, 4 Skills 1, 2, 5	Range 1, 2, 3 Skills 1, 2,
NC/NLS Y2T2	3d 3e	T16 S7 S9 W10	T21	T16 S1 W10

Fireflies

Stage 7

Sue Calcutt

Teaching Notes

Contents

Introduction

Fireflies is an exciting non-fiction series within *Oxford Reading Tree*. The books are specially designed to be used alongside the Stage 1 stories. They provide practice of reading skills in a non-fiction context whilst using the same simple, repetitive sentences as the *Oxford Reading Tree* stories. They also contain a selection of high frequency vocabulary. Each stage builds on the reading skills and vocabulary from previous stages, and helps children to read with growing confidence. As children read these books, they should be encouraged to read independently through: using their knowledge of letter sounds; learning to recognize high frequency words on sight; using the pictures and the sense of the story to work out new vocabulary.

To help children approach each new book in this stage with confidence, prepare the children for reading by talking about the book, asking questions and using these Teacher's Notes and the additional *Guided Reading Cards* and *Take-Home Cards*.

How to introduce the books

Before reading the book, always read the title and talk about the picture on the cover. Go through the book together, looking at the pictures and talking about them. If there are words that are new or unfamiliar, point them out and read them with the children.

This booklet provides suggestions for using the books with groups of children or individuals. You can use the ideas with shared, group or guided reading sessions, or with individual children. Suggestions are also provided for writing, speaking and listening and cross-curricular links. You can use these suggestions to follow on from your reading, or use at another time.

Guided Reading Cards are available for each book. These provide more detailed guidance for using the books for guided reading. *Take-Home Cards* are also available for each book. These provide prompts and suggestions for parents reading with their children. You can store the relevant card with each book in your "Take-Home" selection of titles.

Glorious Mud				
Scotland	Listening/Talking Level A	Level A/B	Level A/B	Level A/B
N. Ireland	Activities a, f, g Outcomes a, b, e, g	Activities a, b Outcomes b, c, d, e, f, g	Opportunities a Outcomes b	Activities a, b Outcomes b, c, d, f
Wales	Oracy Range 1, 3 Skills 1, 2, 5	Range 1, 2, 3 Skills 1, 2, 4	Range 1, 2, 4 Skills 1, 2, 5	Range 1, 2, 3, 4 Skills 1, 2, 4
NC/NLS Y2T2	1e	T19 S8 W4	W21	T15 S1 W4 W10
What Do You Want To Be?				
Scotland	Listening/Talking Level A	Level A/B	Level A/B	Level A/B
N. Ireland	Activities a, f, g, i Outcomes a, b, c, d, e, g, i	Activities a, b Outcomes b, c, d, e, h	Opportunities a Outcomes a, b, c	Activities a, b Outcomes b, c, d, e, f
Wales	Oracy Range 1, 2, 3 Skills 1, 2, 3, 4, 5, 6	Range 1, 2, 3 Skills 1, 2, 4	Range 1, 2, 4 Skills 1, 4, 7	Range 1, 2, 3 Skills 1, 2
NC/NLS Y2T2	10c	T17 T19 S1 S9 W5 W10	S9	T2 T17 S9

Making a Space Shuttle

Reading the book with individuals or guided reading groups

NB for additional and more detailed guidance on guided reading see Stage 7 Guided Reading Cards (available separately, ISBN 019919792X). Take-Home Cards are also available, providing guidance for parents/carers (ISBN 0199197911).

Introducing the book

- In examining the title and cover of this book, establish with the children its likely content.
- Read the blurb on the back of the book and use this to support predictions.
- Explain that this book contains instructions as well as information they will find useful about space and space travel.
- Tell them that they will encounter many new specialist words, which they may include in their class dictionary or personal glossary later on.

During reading

- Remind the children that they need to read from the beginning, as the information about space travel in general and space shuttles will help them understand the second part of the book.
- Ask the children to observe the diagrams or photos and match them to the appropriate text.
  Can they think how the visual aspects of the book support their understanding of the print?
- When reading, can they spot words which have more than two syllables, for example "astronaut" or "atmosphere".

Observing Check that the children:

- read the book from the beginning, and show they are using the visuals to support their understanding (T19)
- are reading multi-syllabic words by maintaining a fluency and understanding (W5)

After reading

- Can the children discuss the nature of a space shuttle and describe some of its components?

- Are they aware of the changes that take place during take-off, and how the shuttle returns to earth?
- Can they show you images from the book which illustrate the above processes?
- Can they share any multi-syllabic words encountered? Would they choose these to enter into their collections of special words?

Group and independent reading activities

Text level work

Objective To use other alphabetically ordered texts, e.g. indexes; to discuss how they are used (T18)

- Ask the children to look at the index at the back of the book. Discuss how this is a list of words which can all be found in the text, and may help someone wanting to find out about that particular aspect of shuttles and space travel.
- Tell the children that you would like them to use the page reference number to track down the whereabouts of each of the words in the index. Can they read the sentence it is included in to help them understand its meaning?

Sentence level work

Objective To re-read own writing and check for sense (S3)
To secure the use of simple sentences in own writing (S9)

- Present the children with some of the words from the index, of which they have tracked and discussed the meaning. Ask them to write their own sentence for each word, re-reading their own writing and checking for sense

Word level work

Objective To discriminate orally syllables in multi-syllabic words. Extend to written forms and note syllable boundary (W5)

- Fold a piece of paper into three columns and ask the children to write at the top of the first column: one syllable; the second: two syllables; the third: three syllables or more. Tell them you want them to scan the text, and select words, deciding which column they should be written in, and then do so. Model the activity by clapping the syllables of some words, and helping the children choose where to write them. Circle the syllable sections as they speak them.

Speaking and listening activities for groups

Objectives   2e) ask questions to clarify their understanding

● Invite the children to share the book with a friend. Encourage the new reader to ask questions about its content and for the experienced reader to give explanations relating to such questions.

● Alternatively children could work in pairs to discuss and then write questions for other children to answer in a comprehension exercise when it is their turn to read the book.

Cross-curricular links
◀▶ **D&T (QCA 2A) Vehicles**
Make the space shuttle model as a project.

Writing

Objectives   To produce simple flow charts or diagrams that explain a process (T21)

After oral and practical exploration of the instructions in this book, the children could prepare a flowchart or diagram, which informs others how to make a space shuttle. This could be in the form of a poster, and include colour and a varied text presentation. Sentence level work completed in an earlier session may be useful here.

Things that Sting

Reading the book with individuals or guided reading groups

NB for additional and more detailed guidance on guided reading see Stage 7 Guided Reading Cards (available separately, ISBN 019919792X). Take-Home Cards are also available, providing guidance for parents/carers (ISBN 0199197911).

Introducing the book

- Look at the cover and see if the children can identify the creature on the front. Tell the children that as they read through the book they will be able to identify it.
- Explain that this book will teach them about a number of stinging things.
- Point out that the book has an index and that this is a list of words written in alphabetical order.

During reading

- Tell the children you would like them to read the book, starting at the Contents page.
- Ask them to look out in particular for pictures of the creature on the front cover and to remember its name when they read about it.
- Remind them to take a look at the index and see what they notice about it.

Observing Check that the children:

- use the Contents page to get a general idea of the range of stinging things they will learn about; use indexes and discuss how they are used (T18)

After reading

- Ask the children if they have managed to identify the creature on the front cover.
- Can they tell you about any of the other stinging things listed in this text?
- What have they noticed about the index? How are the words ordered? And what do all the numbers refer to? Explain how the index works and that they will have a chance to test out the page references.

Group and independent reading activities

Text level work

Objective To use alphabetically ordered texts, e.g. indexes; to discuss how they are used (T18)

- Ask children to find the index page and remind them how each word on the list of words can be found in the text. Can they remember how they can find them in the text?
- Practise tracking the words in the index by selecting one or two and looking at the page numbers.
- Present them with all the words which feature in the index, written on pieces of card, to practise putting them in alphabetical order.
- Discuss how using an index, when searching for information, can be a quick way to find out things.

Sentence level work

Objective To be aware of the need for grammatical agreement, matching verbs to nouns (S4)

- Have sentences written on a flip chart with some words missing, for example: "The bee _____ after it stings." Present children with alternative words to place in the gap: die, dies, died. Can they write in the word that makes sense?
  Other examples: "A jellyfish _____ more than one sting" (had, has, have) "The stings _____down like a curtain of fine threads." (hang, hangs, hung)

Word level work

Objective To discriminate orally syllables in multi-syllabic words (W5)

- Present the children with the following words: sting, scorpion, stingray, dangerous surviving, bee, harmless.
- Practise saying them and clapping the syllabic beat, for example: sting ray – 2 syllables/claps.
- Ask the children to write each word under one of the following headings: one syllable, two syllables, three syllables, etc. Can they circle the parts of the word which make up each syllable?

Speaking and listening activities in groups

Objectives   2e) Ask questions to clarify their understanding

- With adult support, readers can show the book to class members and tell them about its content, looking briefly at some of the pictures.
- On white boards, other class members can write questions they would like to ask about "Things that Sting".
- Have a question and answer session where children practise their speaking and questioning skills.

Cross-curricular links
◀▶ **ICT (NC 1a)**
Gather information from a variety of sources (CD-ROMs)
With appropriate software, conduct a search for information about the "Things that Sting". Print images and text as appropriate and display to support the Speaking and Listening activity, or in a special interest booklet made in the writing activity.

Writing

Objective   To re-read own writing to check for grammatical sense (S2)

- Using images and/or text from the CD-ROM search, children can construct and make a booklet about "Things that Sting".
  In writing about each stinging thing, children can check that sentences make sense, and that verbs are constructed accurately.

Sport Then and Now

Reading the book with individuals or guided reading groups

NB for additional and more detailed guidance on guided reading see Stage 7 Guided Reading Cards (available separately, ISBN 019919792X). Take-Home Cards are also available, providing guidance for parents/carers (ISBN 0199197911).

Introducing the book

- Examine the front cover, establishing the title and author. Discuss the nature of text: non-fiction/information book. Read the blurb on the back of the book and invite children to predict the content and what they might learn from it.
- Point out the long vowel phonemes they will encounter in this text and tell them to look out for such examples as they read.
- Ask children to browse through the text, noting the differences between old and new photographs.
- Can they spot the range of ways text has been presented? For example, can they spot captions, headings and different types of print?
- Explain that although this is an information book, they need to read from the beginning and not just select sections of interest.

During reading

- Tell the children that you would like them to begin reading the Contents page to get an idea about the types of sport this book will teach them about. They can then move on to the introduction and look at the pictures, to spot "then and now" photographs, and match corresponding text captions and charts, etc.
- Encourage the children to read about the other types of sport and the history of them independently or with a partner, seeing if they can spot changes in equipment and clothes.

Observing Check that the children:

- are blending phonemes outlined to read fluently (S2)

After reading

- Can the children tell you of any significant differences in the playing of sport that they have noticed particularly?

- Can they remember the main sports covered in this text?
- How have headings and print type been used to make the information clearer?

Group and independent reading activities

Text level work

Objective To use glossaries to locate words by using initial letter (T16)

- Prepare a set of words which are all part of the Glossary list. Have definitions to hand also and ask children to match them to the words. Invite children to sort words into alphabetical order and then check if they have done this correctly by comparing with the actual Glossary. Remind them to look at the initial letter of each word. Can they find references to each word within the text, by remembering their encounter with these words as they were reading?

Sentence level work

Objective To investigate and recognize a range of ways of presenting texts: bold print captions headings, etc. (T7)

- Present children with plain paper, felt tipped pens and crayons. Ask them to divide the paper into four sections and choose a different sport heading for each section. Can they make the heading bold and colourful? Remind them to give the whole page a title heading. In each section they can write in modest print, a sentence saying what they have learned about that particular sport.

Word level work

Objective To build individual collections of personal interest or significant words (S10)

- Transfer definitions and explanations, along with the actual words studied in the Text level activity into their own personal "Vocabulary Book".

Speaking and listening activities for groups

Objective 2e) Ask questions to clarify their understanding

- The reader can sit with a friend who has not read this particular text. The newcomer to the text can browse through it and be encouraged to ask questions about its content. The child with prior knowledge should attempt to answer questions clearly.

Cross-curricular links
◀▶ **History (NC 4a)**
How to find out about the past from a range of sources of information (pictures and photographs).
History (NC 1a, b)
Place objects in chronological order; use common words and phrases relating to the passing of time.

Writing

Objective To make class dictionaries and glossaries of special interest words, giving explanations and definitions (T2, T20)

- Children can be encouraged to add definitions or explanations relating to new and interesting vocabulary encountered in this text into a class "Special and Interesting Words" book.

Fire

Reading the book with individuals or guided reading groups

NB for additional and more detailed guidance on guided reading see Stage 7 Guided Reading Cards (available separately, ISBN 019919792X). Take-Home Cards are also available, providing guidance for parents/carers (ISBN 0199197911).

Introducing the book

- Discuss the title and probable content of this explanatory text.
- Point out that they will find out about the nature of fire, as well as historical events that have been caused by fire.
- Draw their attention to the Contents page and scan the list with the children.
- Discuss the importance of information read at the beginning, and how it can be needed to understand passages later on in the text.

During reading

- Tell them you would like them to read the text independently
- Ask the children to browse through the book and observe the headings.
- Can they predict when the information on a page will be about a famous fire?
- As they read, ask children to notice words that may be new to them. Ask them to write down the new words, so that they can research their meaning later.

Observing Check that the children:

- browse and scan the headings (S7)
- are making notes of new and unknown words (W10)

After reading

- Ask the children to tell you about the most devastating facts they have encountered in this book.
- Can they remember where some of the most historic fires have broken out?
- Can the children tell you what the plague is?
- Do they have lists of words they wish to investigate further?
- Have they been able to guess at some of these words' meanings by reading ahead?
- Retain the lists for further use.

Group and independent reading activities

Text level work

Objective To use dictionaries and glossaries to locate words by using initial letter (T16)

- Using the lists of words compiled by the children as they read the text independently, present them with the opportunity to research the definition of these words by showing them how to do so using a dictionary.
- Take a word from each child's list, for example "scroll", and establish the initial letter in order to then flick through the dictionary and find the appropriate section. It may be worth ensuring that the dictionaries available for this exercise include the types of vocabulary being investigated.

Sentence level work

Objective To secure the use of simple sentences in own writing (S9)
To recognize a range of ways of presenting texts including headings (S7)

- Children can write a new word as a heading, and its definition as a sentence, in their own personal word book or class dictionary.

Word level work

Objective New words from reading linked to particular topics (W10)

- Given that the children will be investigating and defining quite a few new words from this text, they could make a special "Words about Fire" wall display for the rest of the class to read and learn from.
- Words could be written in bold and eye catching ways and might include additional words, such as: devastating, arsonist, pyromaniac, ignite, wildfire, temperature, damage, raged, etc.

Speaking and listening activities for groups

Objective 3d & 3e) extend their ideas in the light of discussion and give reasons for opinions and actions.

- In engaging in the activities listed in the Cross-curricular links below, the above objectives can be met readily.

Cross-curricular links

PSHE (NC 3g) Rules for and ways of keeping safe

Discuss with the children how they think fires can start in the home. List their ideas, with teacher direction, for keeping safe and avoiding fire. Go on to outline the very important action they should take in the event of a fire. Remind them of the school fire policy and what they should do if they hear the fire bell and why. If possible, include a fire drill.

Science (QCA 2F) Using electricity

In learning about the dangers of electrical items and electricity, children can make posters explicitly referring to the possibility of fire.

History: Significant event in history: The Great Fire of London

Writing

Objective   Produce simple flow charts that explain a process (T21)

● Ideas for development: What to do during a fire drill
Things that can lead to a fire
Action to take if a fire happens in
your home

Glorious Mud

Reading the book with individuals or guided reading groups

NB for additional and more detailed guidance on guided reading see Stage 7 Guided Reading Cards (available separately, ISBN 019919792X). Take-Home Cards are also available, providing guidance for parents/carers (ISBN 0199197911).

Introducing the book

- Discuss the title of this book. Ask, "How can 'Mud' be glorious?" What types of creatures do the children think will enjoy being in and around mud?
- Look at the cover and read the blurb on the back. Establish that this is an explanatory text. What do they think they will learn?
- Consider that this text will teach them how to make and do things and that you would like them to see how the author has used flowcharts to write instructions.
- Remind the children that although this is an information book, they need to read all of it, not just select pages of interest.
- Discuss the importance of information read at the beginning, and how it can be needed to understand passages later on in the text.

During reading

- Start with the Contents page. The children may like to browse through the book, observing the visual elements of the book and in particular any flowcharts or sequenced writing.
- Ask them to look for words which are made up of component parts, for example "tablespoon". This may make some longer words easier to read.

Observing Check that the children:

- are navigating their way around specialized text which presents them with sequenced information or instructions, for example making mud pies on page 15 (T19)

After reading

- Can the children tell you what is "glorious" about mud?
- Can they explain how the illustrations and photos have helped them understand more about mud and the make-up of it?

- Did they learn how to do anything that they would like to try?
- Encourage them to discuss the method of explanation: flowchart, sequential instructions, etc.
- In reading the text, did they notice any compound words, when tackling difficult text?

Group and independent reading activities

Text level work

Objective To read flow charts and cyclical diagrams that explain a process (T19)

- Ask the children to flick through the book and find the examples of instructional writing. They should find: Soil Experiment, Make a Mud Pie, Mud Houses. Focus on "Make a Mud Pie". Children can be given incorrectly ordered instructions which they need to un-jumble and paste into a flowchart on additional paper. They could test out their instructional flowchart by having a go at making the mud pies!

Sentence level work

Objective To use commas to separate items in a list (S8)

- Can the children write a sentence about the Soil Experiment, listing all the things they would need in order to do it, using commas to separate each item.
- Repeat with the other examples of instructional text: Make a Mud Pie, Mud Houses.

Word level work

Objective To split familiar oral and written compound words into their component parts (W4)

- Invite children to conduct a search through the text for compound words. They can write them in their Vocabulary Books or elsewhere, and write the component parts by the side. They should find: "themselves", "warthogs", "classroom", "tight-fitting", "rainwater" "underground", "tablespoon", "topsoil". They can use the text or a dictionary to find definitions of each compound word.

Speaking and listening activities for groups

Objective 1e) include relevant detail

● If children have had the opportunity to try out some of the processes included in the text, invite them to prepare with a friend a report on what they have done. Remind them to explain about the best kind of mud to use for the job and to include details about everything they needed.

Cross-curricular links

◀▶ **Science (QCA 2D)** Grouping and changing materials
Children can explore some of this unit by completing the experiments in mud soil and water observations, and mud manufacturing! In addition they can find out about changes in materials and whether or not they are reversible.

Writing

Objective To produce simple flow charts or diagrams that explain a process (W21)

Ask children to read pages 7 and 8. Can they relate this instructional text to a new reader as a flowchart, with illustrations/diagrams? Provide children with attractive base paper, thin felt tips, and sticky labels for captions.

What Do You Want To Be?

Reading the book with individuals or guided reading groups

NB for additional and more detailed guidance on guided reading see Stage 7 Guided Reading Cards (available separately, ISBN 019919792X). Take-Home Cards are also available, providing guidance for parents/carers (ISBN 0199197911).

Introducing the book

- Discuss with the children the title of this book, establishing that it is in the form of a question. The purpose of the book is to help them answer the question.
- Talk briefly about any ideas the children have about what they would like to be.
- Look through the book and point out the repeated format of the text.
- Explain that they will learn about different kinds of jobs they might choose to do as adults.

During reading

- Tell the children that you would like them to read the book, finding out about all the different kinds of jobs outlined.
- Ask them to notice that each section tells them what opportunities each job would give them, and you would like them to remember these as they read.
- Prompt the children to use pictures and diagrams to help them tackle parts of the text, or new vocabulary.

Observing Check that the children:
- are reading from section to section in turn (T19)
- are finding and reading the word "opportunity" (W5)
- are coping with technical vocabulary relative to any given job, using picture cues to support the sense (W10)

After reading

- Ask the children:
  Has this book helped you to think of a job you might like to do when you grow up?

*Can you tell me what kind of opportunities this job would give you,
and why do you think you would like the job?*
What new words have you read and can you share them with us?

Group and independent reading activities

Text level work

Objective Know that glossaries give definitions and explanations, discuss what definitions are (T17)

- Look at glossaries in other books with the children. Tell them that a glossary is a list of words that occur in the text and their definitions.
- Ask the children to tell you what they think a definition or explanation is.
- Invite children to think of words that they would include in a glossary for *What Do You Want To Be?* What definitions would they give?
- Can the children order the glossary words alphabetically?

Sentence level work

Objective To use awareness of grammar to decipher new words, e.g. to predict from the text (S1)

- Prepare some sentences from the text with one key word masked, for example: "They need to learn how to _____ in spaceships in outer space." Prepare missing key words and make them visible to the children.
- Explain that when the children come across a new word which they don't know how to read, they can pretend it isn't there and read the sentence without it.
- When they have practised this once, ask them to think what the word might be by trying each of the key words in the gap. Can they agree which word makes sense?
- Repeat with other examples of sentences where technical vocabulary might prove difficult, giving them a selection of key words to help them.

Word level work

Objectives To spell common irregular words from Appendix list 1 (S9)

- Ask children to scan the text for the following words: people many would where were school their there house about
- Get them to write the words out and then practise spelling them without looking, using the "Look-cover-spell-check" method.
- Explain the difference between "their" and "there", and ask the children to write a sentence for each one. Repeat for "where" and "were".

Speaking and listening activities for groups

Objective 10c) commenting and reporting

- Having read the text and understood the different jobs described, each child can discuss with a friend what kind of work they would like to do when they grow up.
- Ask each pair to report back to the group their ideal job in the future and to say why they have chosen it.

Cross-curricular links
◀▶ **PSHE (NC 1a, 1b, 52)**
To recognize what they like and dislike; to share their opinions and explain their views; to meet and talk with people
Children can prepare posters and pictures to accompany the speaking and listening activity. Invite visitors into school who can share experiences of one of the jobs outlined in the text.

Writing

Objective To secure the use of simple sentences in own writing (S9)

- Children can choose a member of the working community and write to them, so supporting PSHE links. This can constitute an invitation to come into school and talk about their job of work. It could be someone on-site, such as the caretaker, or someone from a local work place, for example a parent who works at the post office.

Links to other Oxford Reading titles

Fireflies Stage 7	Oxford Reading Tree stories with similar subjects/themes
Making a Space Shuttle	Red Planet, The Flying Machine
Things that Sting	
Sport Then and Now	Poor Old Mum!, Victorian Adventure, Hamid Does His Best
Fire	What Was It Like?
Glorious Mud	The Discovery
What Do You Want To Be?	

OXFORD
UNIVERSITY PRESS

Great Clarendon Street, Oxford OX2 6DP

Oxford University Press is a department of the University of Oxford. It furthers the University's objective of excellence in research, scholarship, and education by publishing worldwide in

Oxford New York

Auckland Bangkok Buenos Aires Cape Town Chennai Dar es Salaam Delhi Hong Kong Istanbul Karachi Kolkata Kuala Lumpur Madrid Melbourne Mexico City Mumbai Nairobi São Paulo Shanghai Taipei Tokyo Toronto

Oxford is a registered trade mark of Oxford University Press in the UK and in certain other countries

© Oxford University Press 2003

The moral rights of the author have been asserted

Database right Oxford University Press (maker)

First published 2003

British Library Cataloguing in Publication Data

Data available

Teacher's Notes: ISBN 0 19 919790 3

10 9 8 7 6 5 4 3 2 1

Page make-up by IFA Design Ltd, Plymouth, Devon

Printed in China through Colorcraft Ltd., Hong Kong